Navigating Life's Triangle
Embracing Life through Validation, Acceptance, and Growth

Afarin Rajaei, Ph.D., LMFT

Growth

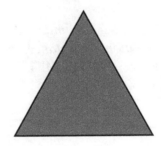

Validation   ## Acceptance

Insightful Reflections Press—San Diego, CA
ISBN: 979-8-3304-2290-6
Title: *Navigating Life's Triangle: Embracing Life Through Validation, Acceptance, and Growth*
Author: Afarin Rajaei, Ph.D., LMFT
Digital distribution | 2024
Paperback | 2024

Published in the United States by New Book Authors Publishing

Dedication

To the wounded child inside me and to all the wounded children within countless beautiful human beings who thought they would be lost in life's wilderness, yet bravely persevered: This is for those who, despite pain and uncertainty, found the courage to show up day after day, seeking truths and meanings in a chaotic world. May we all find peace amidst our struggles, cultivating patience with ourselves and our journey. May we discover purpose in our pain, transforming wounds into wisdom and challenges into growth. In this crazy, beautiful, terrifying, and awe-inspiring life, let us remember that our scars prove our resilience, our story matters, and our presence is significant. To every human being navigating existence: may you find the healing, acceptance, and love you seek, both within yourself and in connection with others.

Table of Contents

Introduction

Dear Friend,

Welcome to this deeply personal exploration of life's joys and sorrows, triumphs and struggles. I'm so grateful our paths have crossed in this way. My name is Afarin, and like you, I am a fellow traveler on this winding road called life. Originally from Iran, I moved to the United States in my early twenties, where I pursued studies in marriage and family therapy, eventually earning a Ph.D. in medical family therapy. Today, I am active in various aspects of my field: I teach at a university, conduct research, run a private online practice, and provide consultations for companies.

As a therapist, I have had the profound privilege of connecting with countless beautiful human beings, each with their unique story. Through these connections, I have come to understand that while our details may differ, we all share a common thread—a longing to feel validated, to make peace with life's inherent unfairness, and to find the strength to keep moving forward.

This book was born from my own messy, imperfect journey and the hard-earned wisdom I've gleaned along the way, both personally and professionally. At its core, it's an invitation—an outstretched hand, a gentle whisper that says, "You are not alone. You matter. And together, we can find a way forward." In these pages, I share brief stories about my clients (with their permission and confidentiality preserved) to illustrate the transformative power of our shared experiences. Their trust has been a privilege and a significant source of my life's learning. To you, the reader, thank you for being here. You, too, are like a star, shining when it's dark.

As we embark on this path of self-discovery, I invite you to consider the chapters ahead as a heartfelt conversation between friends. There will be laughter and tears, moments of profound insight and times when we fumble for the right words. But through it all, we'll remain connected by our shared humanity and our commitment to growing into the fullest, most authentic versions of ourselves.

Our journey will be anchored around a simple yet powerful framework I call "Life's Triangle." Each point on the triangle represents an essential practice for wholehearted living:

1. Validating our experiences
2. Accepting life's inherent unfairness
3. Moving forward with intention

In my work with thousands of individuals, couples, and families, I have noticed a common pattern among those who are unhappy or suffering: a lack of integration of this framework. They tend to focus on only one aspect. For instance, if you only validate your experiences without accepting life as it is, you may experience depression. Conversely, if you accept life as it is without validating your experiences, you might become disconnected from your emotions, leading to a shallow emotional life where neither sadness nor happiness is deeply felt. The third element, moving forward, involves choosing purposeful actions while also validating and accepting your experiences. Focusing solely on moving forward without incorporating validation and acceptance often leads to burnout.

Like a three-legged stool, each element is necessary for balance and stability. Validation without acceptance can leave us stuck in resentment. Acceptance without action can slide into resignation. And forging ahead without honoring our experience is a recipe for burnout. But when we integrate all three, a kind of alchemy occurs—transmuting our pain into purpose, our cynicism into wisdom, our suffering into grace.

This book stands apart from others in the market by offering a holistic, systemic perspective based on social justice. While many existing books focus on a single aspect of personal growth, "Embracing Life's Triangle: Validate, Accept, and Move Forward" integrates all three elements into a cohesive framework. This approach acknowledges the complex interplay of our emotions, challenges, and growth, providing a comprehensive guide to navigating life's intricacies.

In the pages ahead, we'll explore each point on the triangle in depth, weaving together psychological insights, philosophical musings, and deeply personal stories. We'll sit together in the discomfort of life's hardest moments and stand in awe of its breathtaking beauty. And hopefully, along the way, something within you will whisper, "Yes, this is my story too."

I don't have all the answers. I can't promise to take away your pain or hand you a roadmap to an Instagram/TikTok-perfect life. But what I can offer is my presence, my hard-won wisdom, and a space to explore life's big questions with openness and compassion.

So take a deep breath, grab a warm beverage, and let's dive in—not as guru and disciple, but as two kind and weary people, fumbling our way toward the light, one brave step at a time.

With gratitude and love,
Afarin

Note from the Author

This is how you would read about me in a typical book:

Dr. Afarin Rajaei, Ph.D., LMFT, is a medical, marriage and family therapist, educator, and researcher with a unique blend of Eastern and Western perspectives on mental health and personal growth.

Born and raised in Iran, Dr. Rajaei moved to the United States in her early twenties, bringing with her a rich cultural background that informs her holistic approach to therapy and personal development. Her journey as an immigrant has given her firsthand experience in navigating cultural transitions, adapting to change, and finding strength in adversity.

Dr. Rajaei holds a Ph.D. in Medical Family Therapy and is a Licensed Marriage and Family Therapist. Her academic journey in the United States, combined with her Iranian heritage, allows her to bridge diverse cultural viewpoints in her work, offering a truly global perspective on emotional well-being and personal growth.

As an active practitioner in her field, Dr. Rajaei wears many hats:

- She maintains a private online therapy practice, working with individuals, couples, and families from diverse backgrounds.
- As a university professor, she educates and mentors the next generation of therapists,

imparting not just clinical skills but also the importance of cultural competence in mental health care.

- Her research focuses on the intersection of culture, family dynamics, and individual well-being, contributing valuable insights to the field of mental health.
- She is an associate editor in *International Journal of Systemic Therapy.*
- She is the author of *Match Me if You Can*! an educational game for relationships.
- Dr. Rajaei also provides consultations to companies, helping organizations foster more emotionally intelligent and culturally aware work environments.

Throughout her career, Dr. Rajaei has worked with thousands of individuals, each with their unique story, struggle, and strength. These experiences have deeply informed her understanding of the human psyche and the universal yearning for validation, acceptance, and growth.

In this book, Dr. Rajaei distills her professional expertise and personal wisdom into a compassionate guide for navigating life's challenges. Her approach combines evidence-based psychological principles with deep empathy and cultural insight, offering readers a path to more authentic, fulfilling lives.

Dr. Rajaei's work is a testament to her belief in the resilience of the human spirit and the transformative power of self-compassion, mindfulness, and purposeful living. Through her writing, teaching, and clinical work, she continues to inspire individuals to embrace their

truth, accept life's complexities, and move forward with intention and hope.
BUT,

This is how I want to introduce myself:

Hey there! I'm Afarin Rajaei, and I'm excited you've picked up this book. I grew up in Iran and made my way to the US to dive deeper into the mental health field. I got my Ph.D. in medical family therapy from East Carolina University, and now I wear many hats - therapist, educator, researcher, and leader. Why so many roles? Well, I'm passionate about mental health and, more importantly, about human stories. Our stories are as unique as we are, yet they connect us through similar threads of experience - love, hate, sadness, happiness, disappointment - you name it. My colleagues often ask me, "When do you sleep?" while my friends wonder, "When do you work?" I guess that makes me a bit of an artist in how I approach life. Speaking of art, I've recently started dabbling in acting. And you know what? I'm proud of myself. Not because I'm special or anything, but because I try to "experience" as much as I can and show up fully in this crazy life.

My journey has been quite a ride. I started out in a Muslim country, certain about everything - there was definitely a God and a specific way of thinking about life. Then, in my rebellious teen years, I swung to the other extreme - surely there was no God, no nothing. But as I kept growing and questioning, I realized the only thing I wanted to be certain about was uncertainty itself. These days, I have my own way of looking at life, but I know it's just that - a way, not the way. You'll often hear me say "I don't know," sometimes followed by "I hope it's..." Additionally, one of the biggest lessons I've learned is to be comfortable with being uncomfortable. Trust me, it beats having false hope about getting comfortable one day.

I could go on about myself, my story, and my background for hours (just ask my clients! It was a joke. I don't make sessions about myself), but I'll leave you here so you can dive into the book. Oh, and yes - I use humor in the therapy room, classroom, and my leadership role. Not in my studies yet, but who knows what the future holds?

So, let's embark on this journey together. I hope this book offers you insights, comfort, and maybe a chuckle or two along the way.

Part One
Validating Our Truth

Chapter 1
The Power of Validation - Seeing and Being Seen

Dear friend,

In our journey through life, the simple act of being truly seen and heard can be profoundly transformative. Validation is not just about acknowledging someone's words; it's about recognizing their feelings, their experiences, and their humanity. This chapter delves into the power of validation and its impact on our sense of self and our connections with others.

"I just want someone to understand."

It was a sentiment shared by so many of my clients over the years, usually uttered with a potent mix of wistfulness and frustration. One client, Emily, comes to mind. Emily was a bright, accomplished woman who felt invisible in her own life. Despite her successes, she constantly battled a deep sense of loneliness. "I feel like I'm screaming into a void," she told me during one session, her voice quivering with emotion. "No matter what I say or do, it's like no one truly sees me."

Emily's words encapsulated a lifetime of longing—to be truly seen, heard, and accepted. To have the rawness of her experience acknowledged without judgment or minimization. If you've ever poured out your heart to someone, only to be met with blank stares or well-meaning platitudes, then you know the particular sting of

3

invalidation. It's the sinking sensation when your partner responds to your stress with a dismissive "just relax." The flare of anger when a friend meets your excitement with a patronizing "let's not get ahead of ourselves." The frustrated tears when your pain is met with an empty "everything happens for a reason."

Each time, it's as if a little piece of our experience— of our very self—is being erased. When we're consistently met with indifference, correction, or judgment, we begin to doubt our own feelings. We learn to suppress our needs, to push down our truth to maintain superficial peace. Slowly, we start to lose touch with the wisdom of our own heart. Validation, then, becomes not just a balm for the mind, but a crucial practice for maintaining our emotional integrity and deepening our relationships.

But, here's the revolutionary truth: our feelings are not problems to be solved. Our experiences are not inconveniences to be brushed aside. They are sacred messengers from the depths of our being. Wise guides pointing us to what we value, what we need, where we've been hurt and where we long to go.

Validation is the radical practice of honoring our inner life, exactly as it is. It's the courage to show up for our own experience with warmth, curiosity and acceptance. To look at the landscape of our emotions—the soaring peaks and plummeting valleys, the sun-dappled meadows and foreboding forests—and whisper, "yes, I see you. You belong. You matter.

When we validate ourselves, we create space for our whole truth to be held with care. We soothe our frayed nervous systems and strengthen our sense of self-trust. We widen our capacity to weather life's storms with resilience and grace. Put simply, we come home to ourselves.

This kind of self-attunement is a skill that can be learned and cultivated. Like building a muscle or learning an instrument, it requires intention, practice and patience. It means setting aside our well-worn tools of intellectualizing and problem-solving and instead dropping into the raw terrain of our feeling life.

So how do we begin? The same way we build any relationship—with curiosity, openness and tender care. We start by taking a breath and asking ourselves, "what's alive for me right now? Beneath my thoughts and stories, what sensations and emotions are moving through me?" We learn to listen, without agenda, to the subtle cues and quiet whispers of our body and heart.

As we practice validation with ourselves, a funny thing happens. We become more skillful at offering it to others. When a friend shares their excitement or a loved one expresses their pain, we're able to show up with the same warm presence we've cultivated within. We reflect their experience with care: "I hear you. What you're feeling makes sense. I'm here with you." In this way, validation becomes a powerful force for connection and healing in our relationships.

Of course, there will be times when validating is the last thing we feel like doing—for ourselves or others. When we're drowning in our own emotional tsunami or bristling with unexamined judgments. In those moments, the kindest thing we can do is pause, take a breath, and extend some compassion to ourselves. To remember that this too is part of the human experience and to trust that we're doing the best we can.

Because here's the thing: learning to validate, to truly see and accept what is, isn't a linear journey. It's not about perfection or constant emotional attunement. Rather, it's a messy, imperfect, and utterly worthwhile practice. A way of relating to ourselves and each other with just a bit more tenderness and care.

And the dividends are immense. As we learn to honor our own experience, we naturally extend that grace to others. We create relationships and communities where vulnerability is cherished, where empathy is the default, where no feeling or need is too broken or strange. We remember, again and again, the fundamental dignity of being human.

So my dear friend, as we close this chapter, I invite you to begin. Not with grand gestures or sweeping changes, but with the humblest and holiest of acts— turning toward your own experience with acceptance and care. The next time you notice a feeling rising within you, see if you can greet it as you would a welcomed guest. Offer it a seat at the table of your attention and a cup of compassion.

Trust that as you learn to validate your own beautiful, broken humanity, you make space for others to do the same. That in seeing and accepting what is, you create ripples of healing that flow out into a world desperate for compassion.

And if you forget, if you slip back into judgment and resistance, simply begin again. Reconnect to the truth that echoes in the marrow of your bones and beckons from beyond the stars—you are enough. You matter. You belong. Always and forever, just as you are.

With overwhelming love and belief in you,
Afarin

Chapter 2
Befriending Our Emotions - Navigating the
Landscape of the Heart

Dear friend,

In a world that often values rationality and control, emotions can be perceived as inconvenient disruptions. Yet, our emotions are integral to our human experience, offering profound insights into our needs, desires, and inner truths. This chapter explores the transformative journey of befriending our emotions, learning to navigate the landscape of our hearts with compassionate awareness.

"I used to think my emotions were the enemy, something to be controlled or avoided. But now I see they're my allies, my guides."

Sarah walked into my office, eyes downcast, her hands fidgeting in her lap. She was a successful corporate lawyer, known for her sharp intellect and unwavering composure. But today, she looked fragile, like a glass figurine on the verge of shattering.

"I don't know what's wrong with me," she began, her voice barely above a whisper. "I should be happy. I have everything I ever wanted - a great job, a beautiful home, a loving husband. But lately, I feel so... empty. And then, out of nowhere, I get these waves of anger and sadness. I can't control it. I don't even understand it."

We began our work together with mindfulness practices. I encouraged Sarah to spend a few minutes each day tuning into her body and noticing any sensations or emotions that were present. Slowly, she started to notice a tightness in her chest after stressful meetings, a knot in her stomach when overwhelmed, and a heaviness in her heart when remembering arguments. These sensations, she realized, were her body's way of communicating with her. One day, Sarah came into my office with a revelation. "I just let myself feel everything. I didn't try to fix it or push it away. I just sat with it. And you know what? It wasn't as scary as I thought it would be. It was... liberating."

Through our work together, Sarah learned to honor her emotions as wise guides. She practiced self-compassion, set boundaries at work, reached out to her family more often, and allowed herself moments of vulnerability with her husband. As our sessions were coming to an end, Sarah said, "I used to think my emotions were the enemy. But now I see they're my allies, my guides. They're leading me to a deeper, more authentic relationship with myself." Sarah's journey was a testament to the power of befriending our emotions, not as obstacles but as sacred guides lighting the way home.

In the last chapter, we explored the transformative power of validation - the practice of honoring our inner experience with acceptance and care. But for many of us, the idea of turning towards our emotions with openness and curiosity can feel daunting, even downright terrifying. After all, we live in a culture that valorizes rational thinking and emotional control. From a young age, we're taught to suppress our anger, hide our sadness, and push down our fear. We learn that certain feelings are acceptable and others are shameful. That our worth hinges on our ability to "keep it together" and put on a brave face.

But what if I told you that this well-worn path of emotional avoidance is actually the source of much of our suffering? That in our attempts to bypass or control our feelings, we cut ourselves off from the very wisdom and vitality we long for?

Here's the liberating truth: our emotions are not the enemy. They are wise and worthy guides, inviting us into a deeper relationship with ourselves and the world around us. Each feeling that arises - whether pleasant or painful, intense or subtle - carries important information about our needs, our values, and our boundaries. When we learn to befriend the landscape of our heart, to listen to its whispers and honor its aches, we access a wellspring of self-knowledge and resilience.

So how do we begin to cultivate this kind of emotional intimacy? The same way we nurture any new relationship - with patience, presence, and a hefty dose of self-compassion.

Cultivating Emotional Awareness

The first step in befriending our emotions is simply learning to notice them. This may sound obvious, but for many of us, our feelings operate beneath the radar of our conscious awareness. We move through our days on autopilot, reacting to life from a place of habit and conditioning.

Cultivating emotional awareness means slowing down and tuning in. It means developing a kind of sacred curiosity about our inner world. One powerful way to do this is through the practice of mindfulness -

bringing our full attention to the present moment with openness and care.

As we go about our day, we can start to check in with ourselves regularly: "What sensations are alive in my body right now? What emotions are moving through me? What wants my attention?" We might notice a tightness in our chest, a fluttering in our stomach, a heaviness in our heart. We might name the feelings that are present - anxiety, excitement, grief, contentment.

The key here is to observe our experience without judgment or agenda. We're not trying to change or fix anything, simply to cultivate a compassionate awareness. It can be helpful to think of our emotions as passing weather systems - arising, peaking, and dissolving on their own natural rhythms. Our job is simply to witness them with kindness and allow them to be exactly as they are.

Honoring the Wisdom of Our Feelings

As we practice validating our emotions, a deeper layer of the practice is learning to honor the wisdom they contain. Every feeling that arises, no matter how uncomfortable or inconvenient, is a messenger from our deeper self. Beneath the surface of our anger may be a boundary that's been crossed or a need that's gone unmet. Within the folds of our sadness may be an invitation to grieve a loss or release an old story. Inside the chamber of our fear may be a call to summon our courage and take a leap of faith.

When we meet our emotions with curiosity and respect, we start to decode their sacred messages. We might ask ourselves: "What is this feeling trying to tell me? What does it need from me in this moment?"

10

Sometimes, the answer will be clear and actionable - a request for rest, a yearning for connection, a call to stand up for ourselves. Other times, the message will be more subtle, a gentle nudge towards greater self-awareness and compassion.

As we learn to honor our emotions, we also start to develop a more nuanced understanding of them. We see that feelings aren't inherently "good" or "bad," "positive" or "negative." They're simply energy and information, moving through us in service of our growth and healing. An emotion like anger, for example, can be destructive when wielded unconsciously, but it can also be a powerful catalyst for change and justice. Anxiety may feel uncomfortable in the moment, but it can also sharpen our focus and mobilize us to take action.

Of course, honoring our emotions doesn't mean we're at their mercy, acting on every impulse or wallowing in every wave of despair. Sometimes the wisest response to a feeling is simply to be with it, to breathe into it and let it move through us without reactivity. Other times, we may need to set a kind boundary, reach out for support, or channel our emotions into purposeful action.

The point is, when we approach our feelings with respect and discernment, we access a deeper wisdom about how to respond to them skillfully. We learn to dance with the changing tides of our heart, riding the waves of intensity and savoring the moments of calm.

Embracing the Full Spectrum

As we deepen our practice of emotional attunement, it's important to remember that befriending our feelings isn't a sanitized or sentimental affair. It's not about slapping a happy face sticker over our pain or bypassing the messy, uncomfortable parts of the human experience. Rather, it's about developing the capacity to be with the full spectrum of our emotions - the breathtaking beauty and the bone-deep sorrow, the heart-swelling joy and the gut-wrenching grief.

This kind of whole-hearted living requires tremendous courage and self-compassion. It means showing up for ourselves again and again, especially in the moments when we feel most tender and raw. It means learning to soothe our own hurts, to cradle our own broken pieces with gentleness and care.

One of the most powerful ways to cultivate this kind of emotional resilience is through the practice of self-compassion. Pioneered by researcher and psychologist Dr. Kristin Neff, self-compassion involves treating ourselves with the same kindness, care and understanding we would offer to a good friend. It means recognizing that struggle and imperfection are part of the shared human experience and that we all deserve comfort and support, especially in the midst of hardship.

When we're drowning in difficult emotions, self-compassion might sound like a gentle whisper in our own ear: "I'm so sorry you're hurting right now, my love. This is really hard. I'm here with you." It might look like placing a hand on our own heart or giving ourselves a warm hug. It might mean reaching out to a trusted friend or therapist and asking for the care we so deeply need.

As we practice self-compassion, we start to rewire our habitual responses to emotional distress. Instead of criticizing or condemning ourselves for feeling a certain way, we learn to offer ourselves empathy and understanding. Instead of isolating or numbing out when things get tough, we learn to reach for support and connection. Slowly, we start to trust in our own resilience, in our fundamental capacity to hold and care for ourselves through the storms of life.

Closing Reflection

Learning to befriend our emotions is a lifelong practice, one that invites us into an ever-deepening relationship with ourselves and the world around us. It's not about reaching a state of perpetual happiness or eradicating uncomfortable feelings altogether. Rather, it's about developing the capacity to meet our inner life with compassionate awareness, to honor the wisdom of our feelings, and to respond to them with skill and care.

As we close this chapter, I invite you to take a moment to connect with your own emotional landscape. Take a few deep breaths and check in with yourself: What feelings are alive for you right now? What sensations are present in your body? Can you meet them with a spirit of openness and curiosity?

Remember, befriending our emotions is a radical act of self-love and a powerful catalyst for healing and growth. By honoring the wisdom of our feelings, we reconnect with the deepest parts of ourselves - the parts that long for wholeness, for authenticity, for belonging. We start to trust that our emotions aren't obstacles to be overcome, but sacred guides lighting the way home.

And if you forget, if you find yourself slipping back into old patterns of avoidance or self-judgment, simply begin again. Reconnect to the truth that your feelings are valid, your needs matter, and your heart is inherently worthy of love and care.

May you grow ever more skillful in navigating the terrain of your inner world. May you befriend your emotions with fierce tenderness and unwavering compassion. And may you come to trust, more and more each day, in the wisdom of your own wild and precious heart.

With love and solidarity,
Afarin

Chapter 3
The Art of Self-Compassion - Embracing Our Imperfect Humanity

Dear friend,

As we navigate our journey towards acceptance and self-awareness, we often encounter the profound need for self-compassion. In a world that frequently celebrates perfection and relentless perseverance, the act of being kind to ourselves can feel revolutionary. This chapter invites us to explore the art of self-compassion, recognizing and embracing our inherent imperfections.

"I'm so tired. I feel like I'm failing in everything."

Leila sat across from me, her hands clenched in her lap, eyes filled with a mixture of hope and exhaustion. She had moved to the United States five years ago from Iran, chasing the promise of a better life for herself and her young daughter. Back in Iran, she had been a respected engineer, but here, she worked long hours in a bakery to make ends meet while studying at night to revalidate her credentials. "I'm so tired, Dr. Rajaei," she began, her voice barely above a whisper. "I feel like I'm failing in everything. I'm not the mother I want to be, my studies are overwhelming, and I miss my family so much."

We started our work together by exploring the concept of self-compassion. Leila had grown up in a culture where self-sacrifice and perseverance were highly valued, but where self-kindness was often seen as indulgent or weak. She struggled to see how she could be compassionate towards herself without losing her drive and determination. To help her understand, I shared a simple analogy: "Imagine your daughter, tired and overwhelmed, coming to you for comfort. Would you criticize her, or would you hold her and tell her it's okay to feel this way?" Leila's eyes softened at the thought, and she nodded. Her journey towards self-compassion began with small, deliberate steps, like noticing her self-critical thoughts and practicing replacing them with more compassionate responses.

One day, Leila shared a breakthrough moment. "Last week, I was studying late at night, and I just couldn't concentrate. Normally, I would have pushed through, telling myself that failure wasn't an option. But instead, I took a break. I made myself a cup of tea and allowed myself to rest. It felt strange at first, but then I realized how much I needed it." This small act of self-kindness was transformative for Leila. By allowing herself to rest, she managed to recharge and approached her studies with renewed clarity and focus. She began to see that self-compassion wasn't about being lazy or giving up; it was about recognizing her limits and honoring her needs. Through these practices, Leila learned to treat herself with the same compassion she offered others, creating a safe inner harbor from which to navigate the challenges of her new life.

In the last chapter, we explored the transformative practice of befriending our emotions - learning to meet our inner landscape with curiosity, acceptance, and care. At the heart of this practice is a radical shift in the way we relate to ourselves - a movement from judgment and self-criticism to empathy and understanding. This is the essence of self-compassion: treating ourselves with the same kindness and concern we would offer to a dear friend.

For many of us, the concept of self-compassion can feel foreign, even indulgent. We're so used to motivating ourselves through harsh self-talk and relentless striving that the idea of relating to ourselves with gentleness and care can seem like a luxury we can't afford. We worry that if we're too kind to ourselves, we'll lose our edge, become complacent, or let ourselves off the hook for our perceived shortcomings.

But here's the revolutionary truth: self-compassion isn't a weakness; it's a strength. It's not about lowering our standards or letting ourselves off the hook, but about learning to meet our inevitable struggles and imperfections with a more balanced, supportive inner stance. When we cultivate self-compassion, we create a safe inner harbor from which to navigate life's challenges with greater resilience, creativity, and ease.

The Three Elements of Self-Compassion

According to Dr. Kristin Neff, a pioneer in the field of self-compassion research, self-compassion involves three core elements: mindfulness, common humanity, and self-kindness. Let's explore each one in turn.

Mindfulness: At its core, mindfulness is about being present with our experience as it is, without judgment or resistance. In the context of self-compassion, mindfulness means turning toward our painful thoughts and emotions with a spirit of openness and curiosity. Instead of getting caught up in our mental storylines or trying to push away uncomfortable feelings, we learn to simply observe them with a kind, steady attention.

This takes practice, of course. Our minds are wired to fixate on the negative and to rehash the past or worry about the future. But as we cultivate mindfulness, we start to create a bit of space between ourselves and our passing mind states. We learn to relate to our thoughts and emotions as temporary phenomena moving through us, rather than absolute truths that define us. This bit of distance allows us to respond to our inner experience with greater wisdom and care.

Common Humanity: One of the greatest barriers to self-compassion is the belief that we're alone in our struggles - that there's something uniquely flawed or broken about us. We look around and see others seemingly sailing through life, and we conclude that we must be falling short in some fundamental way.

But the truth is, no matter how shiny and curated someone's life may look from the outside, every human being knows the taste of suffering. We all face challenges, make mistakes, and bump up against our limitations. We all feel inadequate, anxious, or overwhelmed at times. This is part of the shared human experience, not a personal failing.

When we recognize our common humanity, we start to feel less isolated and deficient. We see that our struggles are not aberrations to be ashamed of, but natural, inevitable parts of being human. This recognition opens the door to greater compassion, both for ourselves and for others. We start to meet our own imperfections with a sense of humor and forgiveness, knowing that we're all works in progress stumbling toward greater wisdom and love.

Self-Kindness: The final element of self-compassion is perhaps the most radical and transformative: treating ourselves with the same kindness, care, and understanding we would offer to a beloved friend. Instead of mercilessly judging and criticizing ourselves for our shortcomings, we learn to respond to our own pain and struggles with gentleness and support.

In practical terms, this might look like:

- Speaking to ourselves in a warm, supportive tone, especially when we're feeling vulnerable or low. Instead of berating ourselves for a mistake, we might whisper words of encouragement: "I know you did your best, my love. It's okay to be human."
- Giving ourselves the comfort and care we need in difficult moments. This might mean taking a break when we're exhausted, reaching out for support when we're lonely, or drawing a hot bath when we're stressed.
- Celebrating our efforts and progress, no matter how small. Instead of fixating on all the ways we're falling short, we learn to notice and savor the moments of growth, courage, and resilience.

When we make self-kindness a habit, we start to rewire our inner landscape. We create new neural pathways associated with safety, soothing, and care. Over time, self-compassion becomes our default mode of relating to ourselves - a wellspring of inner strength and resilience we can draw on in any moment.

The Ripple Effects of Self-Compassion

Cultivating self-compassion is a deeply personal practice, but its effects ripple out to every area of our lives. When we learn to treat ourselves with kindness and care, we show up in the world in a different way. We're more able to set healthy boundaries, communicate our needs, and navigate conflicts with grace and skill. We're more resilient in the face of setbacks and more able to take risks and pursue our dreams.

Perhaps most importantly, self-compassion allows us to show up for others with greater presence, empathy, and authenticity. When we're at peace with our own imperfections, we're more able to hold space for the struggles and vulnerabilities of those around us. We become a safe harbor for others - a reminder that they, too, are worthy of love and belonging, just as they are.

Closing Reflection

Learning the art of self-compassion is a lifelong practice, one that invites us into a radically new relationship with ourselves. It's not about indulgence or self-pity, but about recognizing our shared humanity and responding to our own struggles with wisdom and care.

As we close this chapter, I invite you to take a moment to offer yourself some kindness. Place a hand on your heart and take a few deep breaths. Whisper to yourself, "I am here for you. You are doing your best. You are enough, just as you are."

Remember, self-compassion is not a destination but a way of being. It's a commitment to showing up for ourselves, again and again, with tenderness and understanding. It's a recognition that our worth is not contingent on our successes or failures, but is inherent in our very being.

May you grow in your capacity to embrace your own beautiful, imperfect humanity. May you learn to meet your struggles and missteps with kindness and care. And may you come to trust that you are worthy of your own love and compassion, now and always.

With deep respect and affection,
Afarin

Chapter 4
Validating Others - The Courage to Listen and Reflect

Dear friend,

In our fast-paced, achievement-oriented world, the simple yet profound act of listening can often be overlooked. Yet, validation—the art of truly hearing and reflecting on the experiences of others—is a cornerstone of meaningful connection. It takes courage to set aside our own perspectives and fully engage with another person's reality. This chapter delves into the power of validation and the transformative effect it can have on our relationships and ourselves.

"I don't understand what's happening. I have everything I thought I wanted, but I feel so disconnected."

Mark sat across from me, his usually confident demeanor replaced by an uncharacteristic vulnerability. As a high-powered executive, he was used to being in control, to having all the answers. But today, he seemed lost, almost childlike in his uncertainty.

"I don't understand what's happening," he began, his voice barely above a whisper. "I have a great career, a beautiful family, everything I thought I wanted. But lately, I feel so... disconnected. It's like I'm going through the motions, but I'm not really there. My wife says I don't listen, my kids say I'm always distracted. I want to be present, I want to connect, but I don't know how."

As Mark spoke, I could see the pain and confusion in his eyes. He was a man accustomed to solving problems, to fixing things. But here he was, facing a challenge that couldn't be resolved with his usual strategies. He was being called to develop a skill that had never been part of his professional toolkit: the ability to truly listen, to validate the experiences of others, and in doing so, to reconnect with his own humanity.

In the previous chapters, we've explored the transformative power of validating our own inner experience - learning to meet ourselves with curiosity, acceptance, and compassion. But as we deepen our practice of self-attunement, a natural question arises: How can we extend this same quality of presence and care to others? How can we become a force for healing and connection in our relationships and communities?

The answer lies in the sacred art of validating others - the willingness to show up for another person's experience with an open heart and a listening ear. When we offer someone the gift of our full, non-judgmental attention, we create a space where they can feel seen, heard, and understood. We communicate, without words, a powerful message: "You matter. Your feelings are valid. You are not alone."

In a world that often feels fragmented and isolating, this kind of authentic, compassionate connection is a rare and precious gift. It has the power to dissolve barriers, heal wounds, and remind us of our shared humanity. And yet, for many of us, the practice of validating others doesn't come naturally. We live in a culture that values quick fixes and surface-level interactions. We're encouraged to give advice, offer reassurance, or steer the conversation toward more comfortable topics.

But true validation requires something more of us. It invites us to set aside our own agendas and judgments and to be fully present with another person's lived reality. It asks us to resist the temptation to minimize or explain away their pain, and instead to honor the depth and complexity of their experience. In short, it takes courage - the courage to listen deeply, to reflect authentically, and to bear witness to the full spectrum of human emotion.

The Core Skills of Validation

So what does it look like to validate another person in practice? While there's no one-size-fits-all formula, there are a few core skills that can help us navigate this tender terrain with greater ease and skill.

Presence: At its core, validation is about being fully present with another person - not just physically, but emotionally and mentally as well. This means setting aside distractions, letting go of our own mental chatter, and bringing our full attention to the person in front of us. It means conveying, through our body language and energy, that we are here, we are listening, and we care.

One simple but powerful way to cultivate presence is through the practice of mindful listening. As the other person is speaking, we can notice when our mind starts to wander or when we feel the urge to interject. Instead of getting caught up in these impulses, we can gently bring our attention back to the speaker, anchoring ourselves in the sound of their voice and the expression on their face. We can silently reaffirm our intention to be fully here, fully open, and fully receptive to their experience.

Empathy: Empathy is the ability to understand and share the feelings of another. It's the capacity to imaginatively step into someone else's shoes and to sense, in our own hearts, the contours of their emotional landscape. When we meet another person with empathy, we communicate a deep sense of understanding and care. We convey that their feelings make sense, that their experience is valid, and that they are not alone in their struggles.

Cultivating empathy requires a willingness to be touched by another person's reality - to let their words and emotions land inside of us, even when it's uncomfortable or unfamiliar. It means resisting the urge to analyze, advise, or fix, and instead to simply be with the other person in their experience. We might silently reflect on times when we've felt similar emotions, or imagine how we might feel in their shoes. The goal is not to equate our experiences, but to find a point of resonance - a sense of shared humanity and understanding.

Reflection: One of the most powerful ways to validate another person is through the skill of reflection - mirroring back the essence of what they've shared in our own words. When we reflect someone's experience with care and precision, we let them know that we've truly heard them - not just the surface content of their words, but the deeper feelings and needs beneath.

Reflection might sound like:
- "It sounds like you're feeling really overwhelmed and alone in this struggle."
- "I'm hearing a lot of sadness and frustration in your voice right now."

- "It seems like this situation has really shaken your sense of trust and safety."

The key is to reflect the other person's experience without judgment, interpretation, or advice.

We're not trying to analyze their situation or offer solutions (unless they specifically ask for it). We're simply holding up a clear, compassionate mirror so they can see their own experience more fully.

Acceptance: At the heart of validation is a deep acceptance of another person's reality, exactly as it is. This doesn't mean we agree with everything they say or do. It simply means we honor the validity of their experience, without trying to change or fix it.

In practical terms, this might look like:

- Resisting the urge to minimize or silver-line the other person's pain. Instead of saying "It's not that bad" or "Everything happens for a reason," we might simply acknowledge, "This is really hard" or "I'm so sorry you're going through this."

- Letting go of the need to give advice or solve the other person's problems (unless they explicitly ask for it). Instead, we trust in their inherent wisdom and resilience. We convey, implicitly or explicitly, "I have faith in your ability to navigate this" or "I'm here to support you in whatever way you need."

- Honoring the other person's autonomy and choice. Instead of pushing our own agenda or opinions, we create a space of deep acceptance and respect. We communicate, "Your feelings are valid, your needs matter, and your choices are yours to make."

When we meet another person with this kind of unconditional acceptance, we offer them a profound gift

- the freedom to be fully themselves, without fear of judgment or rejection. We create a safe harbor where they can rest in the truth of their own experience and find their own way forward.

The Ripple Effects of Validating Others

Learning to validate others is a lifelong practice - one that challenges us to grow in presence, empathy, and acceptance. It requires us to set aside our own agendas and judgments and to be fully available to another's inner world. It invites us into the sacred space of the heart, where we can meet each other in our shared vulnerability and strength.

And yet, for all its challenges, the practice of validating others is also deeply rewarding. When we show up for others with an open heart and a listening ear, we create ripples of healing and connection that extend far beyond the present moment. We become a force for good in our relationships and communities - a reminder that each of us is seen, each of us is worthy, and none of us is alone.

Perhaps most importantly, as we practice validating others, we also deepen our own self-acceptance and compassion. We start to internalize the truth that all feelings are valid, all experiences are worthy of care, and all humans are deserving of love and respect. We learn to meet our own vulnerabilities with greater tenderness and grace.

Closing Reflection

As we close this chapter, I invite you to reflect on your own experiences of being validated (or invalidated) by

27

others. Recall a time when someone truly listened to you, without judgment or agenda. How did it feel to be seen and accepted in that way? What impact did it have on your sense of self and your ability to navigate challenges?

Now, consider how you might bring this same quality of presence and care to your interactions with others. The next time a friend or loved one shares something difficult with you, see if you can meet them with the core skills of validation: presence, empathy, reflection, and acceptance. Notice what shifts when you set aside your own agendas and simply show up with an open heart.

Remember, validating others is not about having all the answers or saying the perfect thing. It's about being fully present, deeply empathetic, and radically accepting of another's lived experience. It's about honoring the sacred story unfolding in front of you and bearing witness to the full spectrum of human emotion.

May you grow in your capacity to offer this profound gift to others. May you become a force for healing and connection in a world that so desperately needs it. And may you come to trust that in seeing and accepting others, you also deepen your own worthiness to be seen and accepted, just as you are.

With gratitude and respect,
Afarin

Part Two
Accepting What Is

Chapter 5

The Wisdom of Acceptance - Finding Peace in the
Midst of Struggle

Dear resilient friend,

As we journey deeper into our exploration of personal growth, we arrive at a crucial crossroads: the practice of acceptance. In our previous chapters, we delved into the power of validation and the importance of honoring our experiences. Now, we face perhaps an even greater challenge - learning to accept what is, even when it's not what we want or expect.

"I've done everything right, and now this crisis threatens to destroy it all. There must be a way to find peace and move forward."

Emma, a successful entrepreneur in her late thirties, came to me in a state of deep distress. The global pandemic had hit her business hard, forcing her to lay off employees and dramatically restructure her operations. As she sat in my office, her frustration was palpable.

"I've worked so hard to build this company," she said, her voice tight with emotion. "I've done everything right, and now this crisis comes along and threatens to destroy it all. I can't accept this. There must be something more I can do, some way to fix this situation."

Emma spent sleepless nights poring over financial reports, desperately seeking a solution that would magically make everything okay. She pushed herself to the brink of exhaustion, trying to control an uncontrollable situation. Her relationships suffered as she withdrew from friends and family, too ashamed to admit the depth of her struggle.

Emma's story is a familiar one. Like many of us, she was caught in the grip of resistance, fighting against a reality she couldn't control. This resistance was not only causing her immense stress but also blinding her to potential opportunities and solutions.

The Nature of Acceptance

Acceptance is not resignation or passive acquiescence. Rather, it's a courageous act of acknowledging reality as it is, without resistance or denial. It's about making peace with the present moment, including all its imperfections and challenges.

This practice becomes particularly vital when we encounter circumstances beyond our control. Life inevitably brings loss, disappointment, and uncertainty. We cannot shield ourselves from the fundamental realities of change, impermanence, and the unpredictability of existence.

The Gifts of Acceptance

When we practice acceptance, we open ourselves to several profound gifts:

1. Peace: As we learn to accept reality, we often find moments of calm amidst the storm. The constant internal

fight against "what is" begins to subside, leaving us with more energy and clarity.

2. Clarity: Acceptance allows us to see our situation more objectively. Instead of being clouded by wishful thinking or catastrophic fears, we can assess our challenges with greater accuracy and insight.

3. Empowerment: Paradoxically, acceptance can make us feel more empowered. By focusing on what we can control - our responses, our adaptability, our resilience - we regain a sense of agency.

4. Connection: As we practice acceptance, we often find the courage to be more vulnerable with others. This authenticity can deepen our relationships and open up new avenues of support and collaboration.

Practicing Acceptance in Daily Life

Here are some practices you can use to cultivate acceptance in your own life:

1. Mindfulness: Practice observing your thoughts and feelings without judgment. Notice when you're resisting reality and gently bring yourself back to the present moment.

2. Gratitude: Regular gratitude practice can shift your focus from what's wrong to what's right, making acceptance easier.

3. Self-Compassion: When you're struggling with acceptance, treat yourself with kindness. Remember that it's natural and human to resist difficult realities.

4. Reframing: Try to find alternative perspectives on your situation. Ask yourself, "What opportunities might this challenge be presenting?"

Closing Reflection

Remember, acceptance is not a destination but an ongoing practice. There will be days when it feels impossible, and that's okay. The invitation is to keep returning to this practice, again and again, with patience and self-compassion.

May you find the courage to accept what is, the wisdom to know what you can change, and the serenity that comes from making peace with reality. In the words of Jack Kornfield, "Peace is not dependent on the absence of challenge, but on the presence of acceptance."

With faith in your journey,
Afarin

Chapter 6

Letting Go - The Freedom of Surrendering to Life

Dear fellow traveler,

In our journey through life, there are moments when we must face the difficult task of letting go. Letting go is not about giving up; it's about freeing ourselves from the weight of past expectations and embracing the potential of who we can become. It is about surrendering to life's natural ebb and flow and trusting that, in doing so, we make space for new possibilities to emerge.

Letting go requires courage. It demands that we release our grip on identities, roles, and plans that no longer serve us, and open ourselves to the unknown. This chapter explores the profound freedom that comes with surrendering to life and the transformative power it holds.

"I've always been the provider, the successful one. Now, I need to let go of who I thought I was supposed to be and embrace who I can become."

James sank into the chair across from me, his shoulders slumped with the weight of his struggles. At 45, he had spent the last two decades building a successful career in finance. But now, that carefully constructed life was crumbling around him.

"I don't know who I am anymore," he confessed, his voice barely above a whisper. "I lost my job six months ago, and despite my best efforts, I can't find another one.

My savings are dwindling, my marriage is strained, and I feel like I'm losing my identity. I've always been the provider, the successful one. Now, I feel like a failure. I can't let go of who I thought I was supposed to be."

As James spoke, I could see the pain of holding on etched in the lines of his face. He was clinging to an image of himself, a life plan that no longer fit the reality he was facing. His story illuminated the profound challenge and necessity of letting go - not as an act of giving up, but as a courageous step towards embracing a new chapter of life.

In the previous chapter, we discovered the wisdom of acceptance - the radical practice of meeting reality as it is, without resistance or denial. We explored how acceptance can bring greater peace, clarity, empowerment, and connection into our lives, even in the midst of struggle and uncertainty.

As we deepen our practice of acceptance, we naturally bump up against the next invitation on the path: the art of letting go. Letting go is the courageous act of releasing our grip on the things we cannot control, the stories we've outgrown, and the identities that no longer serve us. It's the practice of surrendering to the flow of life, trusting that we have the resilience and the resources to meet whatever arises.

In a culture that often equates letting go with giving up, this practice can feel counterintuitive, even frightening. We may fear that if we loosen our grip on the reins of control, we'll be swept away by the currents of chaos and uncertainty. We may worry that if we let go of our familiar patterns and defenses, we'll be left vulnerable and exposed.

And yet, as anyone who has ever tried to swim upstream against a powerful current knows, the more we resist the flow of life, the more exhausted and battered we become. The more we cling to our limited ideas of who we are and how things should be, the more we cut ourselves off from the boundless possibilities of growth and transformation.

In the words of the Tao Te Ching, an ancient Chinese text of wisdom:

"Life is a series of natural and spontaneous changes. Don't resist them - that only creates sorrow. Let reality be reality. Let things flow naturally forward in whatever way they like."

When we practice letting go, we align ourselves with this fundamental truth of existence - that change is the only constant, and that our true nature is not fixed or static, but fluid and ever-unfolding. We discover that, far from leaving us vulnerable or unmoored, letting go actually frees us to be more authentically ourselves. It creates space for new possibilities, insights, and ways of being to emerge.

The Layers of Letting Go

Letting go is a practice that operates on many levels - from the most concrete and mundane to the most profound and existential. At its essence, it's about releasing our attachment to the things that hold us back from living with greater freedom, authenticity, and joy.

Some common layers of letting go include:

Possessions: In a culture that often equates worth with wealth, it's easy to get caught up in the pursuit of more - more stuff, more status, more security. But the truth is, our possessions can often weigh us down, both physically and psychologically. They can keep us tethered to a particular identity or lifestyle, even when our hearts are calling us in a different direction. Practicing letting go in this arena might look like decluttering our space, donating items we no longer use, or simplifying our lifestyle to align with our deepest values.

Relationships: Some of the most painful and transformative experiences of letting go occur in the context of relationships. Whether it's the end of a romantic partnership, the loss of a friendship, or the death of a loved one, these moments invite us to release our grip on the way we thought things would be and to open ourselves to new forms of love and connection. Letting go in relationships might also mean setting healthy boundaries, forgiving past hurts, or releasing toxic dynamics that no longer serve us.

Beliefs and Identities: As we move through life, we often accumulate a set of beliefs and identities that shape our sense of self and our place in the world. But as we grow and change, some of these old stories may no longer fit the truth of who we are becoming. Practicing letting go in this arena might look like questioning long-held assumptions, releasing self-limiting beliefs, or allowing ourselves to evolve beyond the labels and roles we've been assigned.

Control: Perhaps the most fundamental layer of letting go is the release of our illusion of control. As much as we may try to plan, predict, and manipulate our lives, the truth is that much of what happens is beyond our sphere of influence. When we cling too tightly to our need for control, we create unnecessary stress and anxiety for ourselves. But when we practice letting go, we learn to surf the waves of change with greater ease and resilience. We discover that, even in the midst of uncertainty, we have the capacity to find moments of peace, purpose, and even joy.

The Gifts of Letting Go

Just as acceptance brings its own unique blessings, the practice of letting go also bears profound fruit in our lives. Some of the gifts of letting go include:

Freedom: When we release our grip on the things that hold us back, we create space for greater freedom and authenticity in our lives. We're no longer bound by the limitations of our past experiences, beliefs, or identities. We're free to explore new possibilities, to follow our deepest callings, and to show up more fully as ourselves.

Resilience: Letting go is a powerful practice for building resilience - the capacity to bounce back from adversity and to adapt to change with grace and flexibility. When we learn to release our attachment to specific outcomes or ways of being, we develop a greater trust in our ability to handle whatever arises. We become more skillful at navigating the ups and downs of life with equanimity and self-compassion.

Connection: One of the paradoxes of letting go is that, even as we release our grip on others, we often find ourselves more deeply connected to them. When we let go of our need to control or change the people in our lives, we create space for more authentic and compassionate relationships to emerge. We're able to meet others where they are, without judgment or agenda. We discover the joy of loving and being loved for who we truly are.

Growth: Letting go is a necessary part of the growth process. Just as trees must shed their leaves in order to make way for new growth, we too must release the old to create space for the new. When we cling too tightly to our familiar patterns and identities, we limit our capacity for transformation. But when we practice letting go, we open ourselves to the natural process of evolution and change. We trust that, even as we release what no longer serves, we are making way for something even more beautiful to emerge.

Practicing Letting Go in Daily Life

Like acceptance, letting go is a practice that we can cultivate in our daily lives through a variety of tools and strategies. Here are a few practices to get you started:

Mindfulness: As we explored in the previous chapter, mindfulness is a powerful tool for meeting reality as it is, without judgment or resistance. When we bring this same quality of mindful awareness to the process of letting go, we start to notice the subtle ways in which we cling to control, to outdated beliefs, or to limiting identities. We learn to observe these patterns with curiosity and compassion, rather than getting caught up in them. Over time, this practice of mindful observation can naturally lead to a greater capacity for release and surrender.

Gratitude: Gratitude is another powerful ally in the practice of letting go. When we intentionally focus on the blessings and abundance that are already present in our lives, we start to loosen our grip on the things we think we need in order to be happy or fulfilled. We develop a greater sense of trust and sufficiency, knowing that we have access to the inner resources we need to meet whatever arises. Practicing gratitude in moments of loss or transition can be especially powerful, reminding us that even as we let go of one thing, we are making space for new blessings to emerge.

Self-Compassion: As we practice letting go, it's important to meet ourselves with kindness and understanding along the way. Releasing our grip on familiar patterns and identities can be uncomfortable, even painful at times. We may experience fear, grief, or a sense of groundlessness as we step into the unknown. In these moments, self-compassion can be a powerful balm. By offering ourselves the same care and tenderness we would extend to a dear friend, we create a safe container in which to navigate the challenges of growth and change.

Ritual and Ceremony: Sometimes, letting go requires a more intentional and embodied approach. This is where ritual and ceremony can be particularly powerful. Whether it's writing a letter to an old belief and burning it in a fire, creating a sacred space to honor a lost loved one, or engaging in a physical practice like yoga or dance to release stuck energy, ritual helps us to concretize the process of letting go. It allows us to engage our whole selves - body, mind, and spirit - in the act of release and renewal.

Closing Reflection

As we come to the end of this chapter, I invite you to take a moment to reflect on your own relationship to letting go. What are the areas of your life where you feel most stuck or stagnant? What are the beliefs, patterns, or identities that may be holding you back from living with greater freedom and authenticity? What might it look like to practice letting go in these areas, even in small ways?

Remember, letting go is not a one-time event, but an ongoing practice - a way of relating to ourselves and the world with greater ease, resilience, and trust. It's a courageous act of faith, a willingness to release our grip on the familiar in order to make space for new possibilities to emerge.

As you navigate the challenges and opportunities of your own letting go process, know that you are not alone. The path of growth and transformation is one that countless others have walked before you, and will continue to walk long after you. Draw strength and inspiration from their example, and trust in your own innate capacity for resilience and renewal.

And if you find yourself struggling along the way, remember to meet yourself with compassion and care. Letting go is a vulnerable and tender process, one that requires patience, persistence, and a whole lot of self-love. Be gentle with yourself as you navigate the ups and downs, and know that each act of release is a powerful step toward greater freedom and wholeness.

May you find the courage to let go of what no longer serves, and to open yourself to the boundless possibilities of growth and transformation. May you trust in the resilience of your spirit, and in the fundamental goodness of life itself. And may you discover, in the spaciousness of surrender, a deeper sense of peace, purpose, and connection.

With boundless faith in your unfolding,
Afarin

Chapter 7

The Gifts of Imperfection - Befriending Our Flaws
and Limitations

Dear friend,

As we continue our journey of acceptance and letting go, we find ourselves face-to-face with one of the most challenging yet liberating truths of the human experience: our inherent imperfection. In a world that often celebrates flawlessness and relentlessly pursues perfection, embracing our flaws and limitations can feel like a radical act of rebellion.

And yet, it is precisely in this embrace of our imperfections that we find some of life's most profound gifts. When we learn to befriend our flaws, to see our limitations not as barriers but as doorways to growth, we unlock a wellspring of authenticity, creativity, and connection that has the power to transform our lives.

"I've always prided myself on being perfect, on never letting anyone down. Now, I'm learning to embrace my imperfections and see them as opportunities for growth and deeper connection."

Olivia sat in my office, her posture perfect and her appearance immaculate, but her eyes betrayed a deep weariness. As a renowned surgeon, she had built her life and career on the pursuit of excellence. But today, that pursuit seemed to be eating her alive.

"I made a mistake in surgery last week," she began, her voice barely audible. "The patient is fine, but I can't stop thinking about it. I've always prided myself on being perfect, on never letting anyone down. But lately, I feel like I'm constantly falling short. At work, at home, with my kids... I'm terrified of making another mistake, of someone seeing that I'm not as perfect as they think I am."

As Olivia spoke, I could see the toll that her relentless pursuit of perfection was taking on her. Her fear of imperfection had become a prison, cutting her off from genuine connection and joy. Her story highlighted the exhausting and ultimately futile nature of trying to be perfect, and the profound need to embrace our human flaws and limitations.

The Myth of Perfection

Before we dive into the gifts of imperfection, it's important to recognize the pervasive and often toxic myth of perfection that permeates our culture. From airbrushed magazine covers to carefully curated social media feeds, we're constantly bombarded with images of idealized beauty, success, and happiness. We're told, explicitly and implicitly, that if we just try hard enough, if we just achieve enough, if we just look good enough, then we'll finally be worthy of love and belonging.

This pursuit of perfection can manifest in many ways:

- The relentless drive to achieve, always pushing ourselves to do more, be more, accomplish more.
- The obsession with physical appearance, constantly trying to mold our bodies to fit an impossible ideal.

- The fear of making mistakes or showing vulnerability, hiding our true selves behind a mask of competence and control.
- The tendency to compare ourselves to others, always finding ourselves lacking in some way.

The problem with this pursuit of perfection is that it's not only exhausting and unsustainable, but it's also fundamentally at odds with our nature as human beings. We are, by definition, imperfect creatures. We make mistakes. We have flaws. We struggle and stumble. This is not a defect to be corrected, but a fundamental aspect of our humanity to be embraced.

The Gifts of Imperfection

When we learn to befriend our imperfections, we open ourselves to a host of unexpected gifts. Here are just a few:

Authenticity: When we let go of the need to be perfect, we create space for our true selves to emerge. We no longer feel the need to hide our flaws or pretend to be something we're not. This authenticity is not only freeing for us, but it's also magnetic to others. It invites genuine connection and creates a safe space for others to be themselves as well.

Creativity: Perfectionism is often the enemy of creativity. When we're too focused on getting things "right," we stifle our natural impulse to explore, experiment, and play. But when we embrace our imperfections, we give ourselves permission to take risks, to make mistakes, and to learn from them. This is where true creativity and innovation flourish.

Resilience: Paradoxically, embracing our imperfections actually makes us more resilient in the face of life's challenges. When we accept that mistakes and setbacks are a natural part of the human experience, we're better equipped to bounce back from adversity. We develop a growth mindset, seeing failures not as permanent reflections of our worth, but as opportunities for learning and growth.

Compassion: As we learn to be kinder to ourselves about our own flaws and limitations, we naturally extend that same compassion to others. We recognize the shared humanity in our struggles and imperfections. This deepens our connections and allows for more authentic, empathetic relationships.

Freedom: Perhaps the greatest gift of embracing our imperfections is the freedom it brings. When we let go of the need to be perfect, we free up enormous amounts of energy that we can channel into living more fully, loving more deeply, and pursuing what truly matters to us.

Practices for Embracing Imperfection

So how do we begin to cultivate this radical acceptance of our imperfections? Here are a few practices to get you started:

Self-Compassion: As we've explored in previous chapters, self-compassion is a powerful tool for meeting ourselves with kindness and understanding. When you notice yourself slipping into self-criticism or perfectionism, try placing a hand on your heart and offering yourself words of comfort and care. "It's okay to be imperfect. I'm doing the best I can."

Vulnerability: Practice sharing your true self with others, including your struggles and imperfections. Start small, with people you trust, and notice how this authenticity often deepens connection and invites others to do the same.

Mindfulness: Use mindfulness to observe your perfectionist tendencies without judgment. Notice when you're caught in the grip of "never enough" thinking, and gently bring your attention back to the present moment.

Gratitude for Imperfection: Try keeping a "gift of imperfection" journal, where you reflect on how your flaws and limitations have actually enriched your life in some way. Maybe a mistake led to an unexpected opportunity, or a perceived weakness became a source of connection with others.

Celebrate Small Wins: Instead of always focusing on what's lacking or what you haven't achieved, take time to acknowledge and celebrate your efforts and small victories along the way.

Closing Reflection

As we close this chapter, I invite you to reflect on your own relationship with imperfection. What are the areas of your life where you tend to hold yourself to impossibly high standards? How might embracing your imperfections in these areas actually lead to greater freedom, authenticity, and joy?

Remember, befriending our flaws and limitations is not about lowering our standards or giving up on growth. It's about recognizing our inherent worth and dignity as human beings, separate from our achievements or appearance. It's about cultivating a kinder, more compassionate relationship with ourselves and others.

As you continue on this journey of embracing imperfection, know that you are not alone. Every human being on this planet is walking their own path of growth and self-acceptance. Draw strength from this shared experience, and trust that as you learn to love your own imperfect self more fully, you create ripples of healing and authenticity that extend far beyond you.

May you find the courage to let your imperfections shine. May you discover the freedom and joy that come from being authentically, beautifully, imperfectly you. And may you extend that same grace and acceptance to all the wonderfully flawed humans you encounter along the way.

With deep appreciation for your perfectly imperfect self,

Afarin

Chapter 8

Dancing with Uncertainty - Cultivating Resilience in
Times of Change

Dear fellow traveler,

In our journey through life, one thing is certain:
change is constant. From the smallest shifts in our
daily routines to the seismic upheavals that reshape
our world, we are continually called to navigate the
unpredictable currents of existence. And yet, for many of
us, uncertainty can feel deeply uncomfortable, even
terrifying. We long for stability, for control, for the
reassurance that we know what's coming next.

But what if, instead of resisting uncertainty, we could
learn to dance with it? What if we could cultivate a kind
of inner resilience that allows us to stay grounded and
open-hearted, even in the face of life's greatest
challenges and changes? This is the invitation of this
chapter - to explore how we can develop a more flexible,
adaptive relationship with the inherent uncertainty of
life.

"I have no idea what I'm going to do. But I'm
learning to adapt, embrace uncertainty, and find new
opportunities in this changing landscape."

Alex slouched in the chair, his youthful face etched
with worry lines that seemed out of place. At 22, he had
just graduated from college, full of dreams and plans for

his future. But now, those carefully laid plans lay in ruins around him.

"Everything's so uncertain," he said, his voice trembling slightly. "I had a job lined up, an apartment picked out... and then the pandemic hit. Now the job offer's been rescinded, I'm living back with my parents, and I have no idea what I'm going to do. I feel like I'm standing on quicksand, and I don't know how to move forward when everything keeps changing."

As Alex spoke, I could sense the fear and confusion swirling within him. He had entered adulthood expecting a clear path forward, only to find himself navigating a landscape of profound uncertainty. His story embodied the challenge we all face in times of rapid change and upheaval - how to find our footing when the ground beneath us keeps shifting.

The Nature of Uncertainty

Before we dive into strategies for cultivating resilience, it's important to understand the nature of uncertainty and why it can feel so challenging. At its core, uncertainty triggers our most primal fears - the fear of the unknown, the fear of loss, the fear of not being able to cope. When we can't predict or control what's coming next, our nervous systems often go into high alert, triggering the fight, flight, or freeze response.

This reaction made perfect sense for our ancestors facing immediate physical threats. But in our modern world, where change is constant and many of our challenges are more complex and long-term, this stress response can become chronic. We find ourselves caught in cycles of anxiety, rumination, and reactivity that drain our energy and diminish our capacity to respond skillfully to life's challenges.

Moreover, our culture often reinforces the illusion that we should be able to control and predict everything in our lives. We're encouraged to plan, to prepare, to have everything figured out. While some degree of planning is certainly helpful, this mindset can leave us ill-equipped to handle the inevitable surprises and shifts that life brings.

The Gifts of Uncertainty

And yet, for all its challenges, uncertainty also brings profound gifts. When we learn to embrace rather than resist the unknown, we open ourselves to:

Growth and Learning: Uncertainty is the fertile ground in which growth occurs. It's in the moments of not knowing, of stepping into new territory, that we discover our strengths, develop new skills, and expand our understanding of ourselves and the world.

Creativity and Innovation: When the familiar paths are disrupted, we're called to think outside the box, to imagine new possibilities. Some of the most groundbreaking discoveries and creations have emerged from periods of great uncertainty and change.

Presence and Aliveness: Uncertainty has a way of bringing us into the present moment. When we can't rely on our usual scripts and predictions, we're called to be more fully awake and engaged with what's actually happening right now.

Flexibility and Adaptability: As we learn to navigate uncertainty, we develop greater mental and emotional flexibility. We become more adaptable, more resilient in the face of change.

Connection and Compassion: Shared uncertainty can be a powerful connector. When we acknowledge our shared vulnerability in the face of life's unpredictability, we often find deeper empathy and compassion for ourselves and others.

Cultivating Resilience in the Face of Uncertainty

So how do we develop the capacity to dance with uncertainty, to stay grounded and open-hearted even when the ground beneath us is shifting? Here are some practices to explore:

Mindfulness: As we've explored in previous chapters, mindfulness is a powerful tool for staying present with our experience, without getting caught up in anxious projections about the future. When you notice yourself spinning out into worry or reactivity, try bringing your attention back to the present moment. Feel your feet on the ground, notice your breath moving in and out. Remember that right here, right now, you are okay.

Self-Compassion: Uncertainty can trigger a lot of self-doubt and harsh self-judgment. Practice meeting yourself with kindness and understanding, especially when you're feeling vulnerable or overwhelmed. Remind yourself that it's okay to not have all the answers, that you're doing the best you can with the information you have.

Cultivate a Growth Mindset: Instead of seeing challenges and setbacks as threats, try viewing them as opportunities for learning and growth. Ask yourself, "What can I learn from this situation? How might this be an opportunity for me to develop new skills or perspectives?"

Build Your Support Network: We're not meant to navigate uncertainty alone. Cultivate relationships with people who can offer emotional support, practical help, and different perspectives when you're facing challenges. Remember, asking for help is a sign of strength, not weakness.

Practice Flexibility: In your daily life, try intentionally doing things differently sometimes. Take a new route to work, try a new hobby, or engage with people outside your usual social circle. This helps build your "flexibility muscles," making it easier to adapt when bigger changes come along.

Focus on What You Can Control: When facing uncertainty, it's easy to get caught up in all the "what ifs." Instead, try focusing your energy on the things you can influence. What small actions can you take today that align with your values and move you in a positive direction?

Cultivate Trust: This might be trust in a higher power, trust in the fundamental goodness of life, or simply trust in your own capacity to handle whatever comes. Reflect on past challenges you've overcome - what inner resources did you draw upon? How can you cultivate more trust in those resources?

Practice Gratitude: Regularly acknowledging the good in your life can help build a sense of resilience and perspective. Even (especially) in difficult times, try noting a few things each day that you're grateful for.

Closing Reflection

As we close this chapter, I invite you to reflect on your own relationship with uncertainty. What are the areas of your life where you struggle most with the unknown? How might embracing uncertainty in these areas actually open up new possibilities for growth and aliveness?

Remember, learning to dance with uncertainty is a lifelong practice. There will be days when you feel graceful and in flow, and others when you stumble and struggle. Be patient with yourself. Trust that each time you choose to stay open in the face of the unknown, you're building your capacity for resilience and adaptability.

May you find the courage to embrace the mysteries of life with an open heart. May you discover, in the midst of uncertainty, a deeper trust in your own capacity to navigate whatever comes. And may you dance with the ever-changing rhythms of existence, finding joy and growth in the journey.

With faith in your resilience and adaptability,
Afarin

Part Three
Moving Forward with Intention

Chapter 9
Clarifying Our Values - Discovering What Matters Most

Dear friend,

As we've journeyed through the practices of validation and acceptance, we've been laying the groundwork for a more authentic, compassionate way of being. We've explored how to honor our experiences, embrace our imperfections, and dance with uncertainty. Now, as we begin this final section of our journey together, we turn our attention to the question of how we move forward - not just surviving, but truly thriving and living with purpose.

At the heart of this exploration is the practice of clarifying our values - discovering and aligning with what matters most to us. Our values are like an internal compass, guiding our choices and actions even in the midst of life's storms. When we're clear about our values, we have a strong foundation from which to make decisions, set goals, and navigate challenges. We're able to move through life with greater intention and purpose, rather than simply reacting to circumstances or following the expectations of others.

"It's time to discover what truly matters to me and align my life with those values."

Rachel sat across from me, her gaze unfocused as if looking inward. At 38, she had achieved what many would consider a successful life - a high-paying job in finance, a beautiful home, a busy social life. Yet there was a hollowness in her eyes that spoke volumes.

"I don't even know who I am anymore," she confessed, her voice barely above a whisper. "I've spent so long doing what I thought I was supposed to do, chasing the next promotion, the next achievement. But now that I've 'made it', I feel... empty. I look around at my life and I don't recognize myself. What do I really care about? What actually matters to me? I have no idea."

As Rachel spoke, I could sense the profound disorientation she was experiencing. She had climbed the ladder of success only to find it was leaning against the wrong wall. Her story highlighted the crucial importance of clarifying our values - of understanding what truly matters to us beneath the noise of societal expectations and external measures of success.

What Are Values?

Before we dive into the process of clarifying our values, let's take a moment to understand what we mean by "values." Values are not goals or specific achievements, but rather the qualities of being and doing that we hold most important. They're the principles that give our life meaning and direction.

For example, some common values include:
- Authenticity
- Compassion
- Creativity
- Connection
- Growth
- Health
- Justice

- Learning
- Love
- Service

Our values are deeply personal and can evolve over time as we grow and experience life. They're not about what we think we should care about, but what truly resonates in our hearts when we're being honest with ourselves.

The Importance of Clarifying Our Values

Why is it so important to get clear on our values? Here are a few key reasons:

Direction and Purpose: When we're aligned with our values, we have a clearer sense of direction in life. Our values act as a compass, helping us navigate decisions both big and small.

Motivation: Living in alignment with our values gives us a deep sense of fulfillment and motivation. We're more likely to persevere through challenges when we're connected to what truly matters to us.

Authenticity: Clarifying our values helps us live more authentically. We're less likely to be swayed by external pressures or expectations when we're grounded in our own truth.

Resilience: When we're clear on our values, we're better equipped to handle life's ups and downs. Our values provide a stable foundation even when circumstances are changing.

Decision Making: Values clarity simplifies decision making. When faced with a choice, we can ask ourselves, "Which option aligns best with my values?"

Practices for Clarifying Our Values

So how do we go about clarifying our values? Here are some practices to explore:

Reflect on Peak Experiences: Think about times in your life when you've felt most alive, most fulfilled, most like yourself. What was happening in those moments? What qualities were you embodying? These peak experiences often point to our core values.

Consider Your Heroes: Who do you admire most, either in your personal life or in the wider world? What qualities do they embody that you find inspiring? Often, the traits we admire in others reflect our own core values.

Imagine Your Ideal Future: If you could wave a magic wand and create your ideal life, what would it look like? Not just in terms of external circumstances, but how would you be being? What qualities would you be embodying? This vision can offer clues to your values.

Notice Your Pain Points: Sometimes our values become clear when we notice what bothers us most. What situations or behaviors (in yourself or others) tend to trigger strong emotional reactions? Often, these pain points indicate where our values are being violated.

Use a Values List: Sometimes it can be helpful to look at a list of common values and see which ones resonate most strongly with you. As you read through the list, notice which values give you a feeling of excitement or a sense of "Yes, that's important to me!"

Journal Prompts: Spend some time writing in response to prompts like:

- "What do I want to stand for in my life?"
- "When I'm at my best, what qualities am I embodying?"

- "What would I like to be remembered for at the end of my life?"

Create a Values Statement: Once you've identified your core values, try crafting a personal values statement. This might be a few sentences or a paragraph that captures the essence of what matters most to you.

Living Our Values

Of course, clarifying our values is just the first step. The real work comes in aligning our daily choices and actions with these values. This is an ongoing practice, one that requires mindfulness, courage, and often a willingness to step out of our comfort zones.

Here are a few strategies for living our values more fully:

Set Intentions: Each morning, take a moment to connect with your values and set an intention for how you want to embody them that day.

Make Value-Based Decisions: When faced with a choice, big or small, pause and ask yourself, "Which option aligns best with my values?"

Regular Check-Ins: Schedule regular times (perhaps weekly or monthly) to reflect on how well your actions have been aligning with your values. Celebrate the times when you've lived your values fully, and compassionately explore the times when you've fallen short.

Surround Yourself with Support: Share your values with trusted friends or family members. Ask for their support in living these values more fully.

Practice Self-Compassion: Remember, living our values is a practice, not a destination. There will be times when we fall short. Meet these moments with kindness and see them as opportunities for learning and growth.

Closing Reflection

As we close this chapter, I invite you to take some time to reflect on your own values. What qualities of being and doing are most important to you? How might your life look different if you were living in even fuller alignment with these values?

Remember, clarifying our values is not about adding another "should" to our lives. It's about connecting with what truly matters to us, what brings us alive and gives our life meaning. It's about creating a life that feels authentic and purposeful, even in the face of life's challenges and uncertainties.

May you find clarity and courage as you explore your values. May you discover, in this exploration, a deeper sense of purpose and direction. And may you move forward with the confidence that comes from knowing and living your truth.

With faith in your inner wisdom,
Afarin

Chapter 10
Purposeful Action - Aligning Our Choices with Our
Truth

Dear courageous traveler,

In our last chapter, we explored the importance of clarifying our values - discovering what truly matters most to us. Now, we turn our attention to the vital next step: aligning our actions with these values. For it is one thing to know what we stand for, and quite another to live it out in the world.

This chapter is about bridging the gap between our inner truth and our outer reality. It's about making the sometimes challenging, often courageous choices that bring our lives into alignment with our deepest values. This is where the rubber meets the road on our journey of personal growth and transformation.

"It's time to align my actions with my true values and live authentically."

Michael leaned forward in his chair, his eyes intense with a mix of frustration and dawning realization. At 45, he had built a successful career as a corporate lawyer, but something fundamental had shifted within him.

"I'm living someone else's life," he said, the weight of his words hanging heavy in the air. "I've done everything I was supposed to do - got the degree, made partner, provided for my family. But I feel like I'm suffocating. I've always had this passion for environmental issues, but I pushed it aside for the 'practical' path. Now, I'm defending corporations that go against everything I believe in. How did I end up so far from who I really am?"

As Michael spoke, I could see the pain of misalignment etched on his face. He had spent years making choices that didn't reflect his deepest values, and the dissonance had finally become too much to bear. His story underscored the vital importance of aligning our actions with our truth - and the courage it takes to make changes when we realize we've veered off course.

The Power of Purposeful Action

When we take action that's aligned with our values, we tap into a wellspring of energy, motivation, and fulfillment. We move from merely existing to truly living - from going through the motions to engaging fully with life. This kind of purposeful action has the power to:

Create Meaningful Change: When our actions align with our values, we become a force for positive change in our own lives and in the world around us.

Build Self-Trust: Each time we make a choice that honors our values, we strengthen our relationship with ourselves. We build confidence in our ability to live with integrity.

Inspire Others: Living our values visibly can inspire and encourage others to do the same. Our actions ripple out, creating a wider impact than we might imagine.

Increase Resilience: When we're connected to our 'why', we're better able to persist in the face of challenges. Our values provide an anchor during difficult times.

Enhance Well-being: Research has shown that living in alignment with our values contributes significantly to our overall sense of well-being and life satisfaction.

Bridging the Value-Action Gap

Despite the benefits, many of us struggle with what psychologists call the "value-action gap" - the disparity between what we say is important to us and how we actually behave. This gap can occur for various reasons:

- Fear of change or failure
- Ingrained habits and patterns
- External pressures and expectations
- Lack of clarity about how to translate values into specific actions
- Overwhelm or not knowing where to start

Bridging this gap requires intention, courage, and often a willingness to step out of our comfort zones. Here are some strategies to help you move from values clarity to purposeful action:

1. Start Small
Don't feel like you need to revolutionize your entire life overnight. Begin with small, manageable steps that align with your values. For example:

- If you value health, you might start by adding a serving of vegetables to one meal each day.
- If you value creativity, you could commit to spending 10 minutes a day on a creative project.

- If you value connection, you might reach out to one friend or family member each week for a meaningful conversation.

Remember, small actions done consistently can lead to significant change over time.

2. Set Specific, Value-Aligned Goals

While values themselves are not goals, we can set specific goals that help us live our values more fully. Use the SMART criteria (Specific, Measurable, Achievable, Relevant, Time-bound) to create goals that align with your values. For example:

- If you value learning, a SMART goal might be: "I will read one non-fiction book related to my field of interest each month for the next six months."
- If you value environmental stewardship, a goal could be: "I will reduce my household waste by 25% over the next three months by composting and using reusable products."

3. Create Supportive Environments

Our environment has a powerful influence on our behavior. Look for ways to structure your surroundings to support your values-based actions. This might involve:

- Removing temptations or obstacles that make it hard to live your values
- Surrounding yourself with people who share or support your values
- Using visual reminders of your values in your living or working space

4. Practice Mindful Decision-Making

In our day-to-day lives, we make countless decisions. Start bringing more awareness to these choices by pausing before acting and asking yourself:

- "Is this action aligned with my values?"
- "How will I feel about this choice later?"
- "What would my best self do in this situation?"

This practice of mindful decision-making can help us catch ourselves before we act out of habit or impulse, allowing us to make more intentional choices.

5. Cultivate Self-Compassion

Remember, living our values is a practice, not a perfect performance. There will be times when we fall short or make choices that don't align with our deepest truth. In these moments, it's crucial to respond with self-compassion rather than harsh self-judgment.

Acknowledge the difficulty of changing ingrained patterns. Recognize your humanity and the universal nature of struggle. Offer yourself the same kindness and understanding you would offer a good friend. Then, gently recommit to your values and take the next small step forward.

6. Celebrate Progress

Take time to acknowledge and celebrate the moments when you successfully align your actions with your values. This positive reinforcement can help motivate continued growth and change. It also helps to build a positive association with living your values, making it more likely that you'll continue to make aligned choices in the future.

7. Regular Review and Reflection

Set aside time regularly (perhaps weekly or monthly) to reflect on how well your actions have aligned with your values. You might journal about:

- Moments when you felt particularly aligned with your values
- Situations where you struggled to live your values
- Any patterns or insights you notice
- Adjustments you want to make moving forward

This practice of regular reflection helps to keep your values at the forefront of your awareness and allows you to course-correct as needed.

Closing Reflection

As we conclude this chapter, I invite you to consider: What is one small, concrete action you can take this week that aligns with one of your core values? How might you set yourself up for success in taking this action?

Remember, the journey of aligning our actions with our values is ongoing. It's not about perfection, but about consistent, intentional practice. Each choice we make is an opportunity to move closer to living our truth.

May you find the courage to act on what matters most to you. May you trust in the power of small, consistent actions to create meaningful change. And may you experience the deep fulfillment that comes from living a life aligned with your values.

With belief in your capacity for purposeful action,
Afarin

Chapter 11

Overcoming Obstacles - The Power of Perseverance
and Flexibility

Dear resilient friend,

As we've explored in previous chapters, the path of personal growth and living our values is deeply rewarding, but it's not always easy. Inevitably, as we strive to align our actions with our deepest truths, we will encounter obstacles. These challenges might come in the form of external circumstances, internal resistance, or the simple inertia of old habits and patterns.

In this chapter, we'll explore how to navigate these obstacles with a combination of perseverance and flexibility. We'll look at common roadblocks on the path of growth and discuss strategies for overcoming them, all while maintaining our commitment to self-compassion and authenticity.

"I believed so strongly in this vision, but now I'm starting to think I was naive. Maybe I'm just not cut out for this. But I have to find the strength and flexibility to keep pushing forward and adapt to these challenges."

Sophia slumped in her chair, her usual energy noticeably absent. At 32, she had left a stable job to pursue her dream of starting her own eco-friendly clothing line. But now, a year into her venture, she was facing what felt like insurmountable challenges.

"I can't do this anymore," she declared, her voice a mix of frustration and defeat. "Every time I think I'm making progress, something else goes wrong. Supply chain issues, funding problems, production delays... it's one thing after another. I believed so strongly in this vision, but now I'm starting to think I was naive. Maybe I'm just not cut out for this."

As Sophia spoke, I could see the toll that constant setbacks had taken on her spirit. The passion that had once burned so brightly was flickering, threatened by the relentless headwinds she'd encountered. Her story exemplified the grueling nature of pursuing our dreams and the resilience required to keep going when obstacles seem to appear at every turn.

Common Obstacles on the Path

Before we dive into strategies for overcoming obstacles, let's acknowledge some of the common challenges we might face:

1. *Fear and Self-Doubt:* As we step out of our comfort zones, it's natural to experience fear and self-doubt. We might worry that we're not capable of change or fear the unknown consequences of living more authentically.
2. *Resistance from Others:* Sometimes, as we begin to live more aligned with our values, we may face resistance or lack of understanding from those around us. This can be particularly challenging when it involves close relationships.
3. *Setbacks and Failures:* The path of growth is rarely linear. We'll likely experience setbacks and moments of perceived failure as we work to change ingrained patterns.

4. *Overwhelm and Burnout:* Sometimes, in our enthusiasm for change, we might take on too much too quickly, leading to feelings of overwhelm or burnout.
5. *Lack of Resources:* We might face practical obstacles such as lack of time, energy, or financial resources to pursue certain value-aligned actions.
6. *Conflicting Values:* At times, we may find our values seemingly in conflict with each other, making it challenging to determine the best course of action.
7. *Societal Pressures:* Broader societal expectations or norms might sometimes seem at odds with our personal values, creating tension and difficulty.

Strategies for Overcoming Obstacles

Now, let's explore some strategies for navigating these challenges with both perseverance and flexibility:

1. Cultivate a Growth Mindset

A growth mindset, a concept developed by psychologist Carol Dweck, is the belief that our abilities and intelligence can be developed through effort, learning, and persistence. When we approach obstacles with a growth mindset, we see them not as insurmountable barriers, but as opportunities for learning and development.

Practice reframing challenges with language that reflects a growth mindset:

- Instead of "I can't do this," try "I can't do this yet, but I can learn."
- Replace "This is too hard" with "This is challenging, which means I'm growing."

2. Break Big Goals into Smaller Steps

When facing a large obstacle or working towards a significant change, it's easy to feel overwhelmed. Break your larger goals into smaller, manageable steps. This not only makes the process feel more achievable but also allows you to celebrate small victories along the way, building momentum and confidence.

3. Practice Self-Compassion

As we've discussed in earlier chapters, self-compassion is crucial, especially when facing obstacles. Remember that struggle is a universal human experience. Offer yourself the same kindness and understanding you would offer a good friend facing a similar challenge.

Try this self-compassion practice when you're struggling:

- Acknowledge the difficulty: "This is really hard right now."
- Remind yourself of our shared humanity: "Everyone faces challenges. I'm not alone in this."
- Offer yourself words of kindness: "May I be patient with myself as I navigate this obstacle."

4. Seek Support and Community

We don't have to face obstacles alone. Seek out support from friends, family, or professionals who understand and encourage your growth journey. Consider joining or creating a community of like-minded individuals who are also working to live more aligned with their values.

5. Stay Connected to Your 'Why'

When facing obstacles, it's crucial to stay connected to why this change or goal is important to you. Regularly remind yourself of your core values and the vision you have for your life. This can provide motivation and perspective during challenging times.

6. Practice Flexible Persistence

While perseverance is important, it's equally crucial to remain flexible in our approach. If one method isn't working, be willing to adjust your strategy. This doesn't mean giving up on your goals, but rather being adaptable in how you pursue them.

Ask yourself:

- "Is there another way I could approach this challenge?"
- "What can I learn from this setback that might inform a new approach?"

7. Celebrate Progress, Not Just Outcomes

Often, we focus solely on end results and overlook the growth that happens along the way. Make a practice of acknowledging and celebrating your efforts and small wins. This helps to build confidence and motivation, making it easier to persist in the face of obstacles.

8. Practice Mindfulness and Self-Reflection

Regular mindfulness practice can help us become more aware of our thoughts, emotions, and patterns of behavior. This awareness allows us to respond to challenges more skillfully, rather than reacting out of habit.

Set aside time for regular self-reflection. You might journal about:

- Obstacles you're currently facing

- Strategies that have been helpful (or unhelpful) in addressing these challenges
- Insights or lessons you've gained from recent experiences

9. Embrace Failure as a Teacher

Reframe failures or setbacks as valuable learning experiences. After a setback, reflect on:
- What can I learn from this experience?
- How has this challenge helped me grow or gain new insights?
- How can I use this experience to inform my path forward?

10. Practice Radical Acceptance

Sometimes, despite our best efforts, we may not be able to overcome certain obstacles immediately. In these cases, practicing radical acceptance - fully accepting reality as it is without resistance - can be powerful. This doesn't mean we like the situation or that we won't work to change it in the future, but it allows us to stop expending energy fighting against what is, freeing up resources to respond more effectively.

Closing Reflection

As we conclude this chapter, I invite you to reflect on an obstacle you're currently facing in your growth journey. How might you apply some of these strategies to navigate this challenge? What would it look like to approach this obstacle with both perseverance and flexibility?

Remember, facing obstacles is not a sign of failure, but a natural and inevitable part of the growth process.

Each challenge you encounter is an opportunity to deepen your resilience, expand your skills, and reaffirm your commitment to living your values.

May you find the strength to persist in the face of difficulties. May you cultivate the flexibility to adapt when needed. And may you trust in your inherent capacity to grow, learn, and overcome, no matter what obstacles you may face.

With unwavering faith in your resilience,

Afarin

Chapter 12
Celebrating Our Journey - The Importance of
Gratitude and Self- Acknowledgment

Dear courageous traveler,

We've come a long way together. From exploring the power of validation to embracing our imperfections, from clarifying our values to overcoming obstacles, we've navigated the rich and complex terrain of personal growth. As we approach the end of this book, it's important to pause and celebrate - not just the destination, but the entire journey.

In our goal-oriented culture, we often rush from one achievement to the next without taking time to truly appreciate how far we've come. But acknowledging our progress, expressing gratitude for our experiences, and celebrating our growth are vital practices that nourish our spirits and sustain us for the ongoing journey of life.

"I never thought I'd make it this far. A year ago, I felt like my life was falling apart. But sitting here now, I realize how far I've come. I've rebuilt my life, rediscovered parts of myself I'd forgotten. I'm proud of how I've handled it all and grateful for the journey."

Lisa sat across from me, a subtle but noticeable change in her demeanor. Over the past year, I had watched her navigate a painful divorce, career uncertainty, and the challenges of single parenthood.

But today, there was a quiet strength in her posture, a soft light in her eyes that hadn't been there before.

"I never thought I'd make it this far," she mused, a hint of wonder in her voice. "A year ago, I felt like my life was falling apart. I was so focused on everything that was going wrong, everything I had lost. But sitting here now, I realize how far I've come. I've rebuilt my life, rediscovered parts of myself I'd forgotten. It hasn't been easy, but I'm proud of how I've handled it all."

As Lisa spoke, I could sense the profound shift that had occurred within her. She had moved from a place of despair to one of quiet gratitude and self-acknowledgment. Her story beautifully illustrated the importance of pausing to recognize and celebrate our journey, especially the strength we discover in navigating life's challenges.

The Power of Celebration and Gratitude

Celebration and gratitude are not frivolous extras, but essential components of a fulfilling life and a sustainable growth practice. Here's why:

1. *Reinforces Positive Change:* When we celebrate our progress, we reinforce the neural pathways associated with growth and change, making it more likely that we'll continue these positive behaviors.
2. *Boosts Motivation:* Acknowledging how far we've come can provide motivation to keep going, especially when facing challenges.
3. *Increases Well-being:* Research has consistently shown that practices of gratitude and celebration increase overall well-being, life satisfaction, and positive emotions.

4. *Builds Resilience:* Recognizing our growth and the support we've received along the way can build our resilience, helping us face future challenges with greater confidence.
5. *Deepens Self-Trust:* Celebrating our journey helps us recognize our own capacity for growth and change, deepening our trust in ourselves.

Practices for Celebration and Gratitude

Here are some ways to incorporate celebration and gratitude into your growth journey:

1. Keep a Growth Journal
Regularly document your growth journey. This could include:
- Challenges you've overcome
- New insights or perspectives you've gained
- Moments when you've lived your values fully
- Skills or qualities you've developed

Periodically review this journal to remind yourself of how far you've come.

2. Gratitude Practice
Develop a regular gratitude practice. This might involve:
- Writing down three things you're grateful for each day
- Expressing appreciation to others who have supported your journey
- Taking time to savor positive experiences, no matter how small

3. Celebrate Milestones

Set milestones along your growth journey and plan ways to celebrate when you reach them. These celebrations don't have to be grand - they could be as simple as treating yourself to a favorite meal or activity, or sharing your achievement with a supportive friend.

4. Create a 'Wins' Jar

Keep a jar or box where you can add notes about your 'wins' - big or small. Any time you overcome a challenge, make progress towards a goal, or live your values in a meaningful way, write it down and add it to your jar. Periodically (perhaps monthly or quarterly), review these notes to remind yourself of your progress.

5. Reflect on Lessons Learned

Take time to reflect on the lessons you've learned through your challenges and growth experiences. How have these experiences shaped you? What wisdom have you gained that you can carry forward?

6. Share Your Story

Consider sharing your growth journey with others. This could be through conversations with friends, writing a blog, or even speaking at community events. Sharing our stories not only allows us to celebrate our own growth but can also inspire and encourage others.

7. Practice Self-Acknowledgment

Make a habit of acknowledging yourself for your efforts and progress. This might feel uncomfortable at first, especially if you're not used to 'patting yourself on the back.' But self-acknowledgment is a powerful way to build self-trust and motivation. Try saying to yourself, "I'm proud of myself for..." or "I acknowledge myself for..."

8. Create a Growth Timeline

Create a visual representation of your growth journey. This could be a timeline where you mark significant moments of challenge, insight, and progress. Seeing your journey laid out visually can be a powerful reminder of how far you've come.

9. Gratitude Meditation

Try incorporating a gratitude meditation into your routine. Spend a few minutes focusing on things you're grateful for in your growth journey - the challenges that have helped you grow, the support you've received, the strengths you've developed.

10. Pay It Forward

One beautiful way to celebrate your own growth is to support others on their journey. Consider how you might use your experiences and insights to encourage, mentor, or support others who are facing similar challenges.

Closing Reflection

As we come to the end of this book, I invite you to take some time to reflect on your journey. Looking back over the chapters we've explored together:

- What new insights or perspectives have you gained?
- What challenges have you faced, and how have you grown through them?

- How have you seen yourself living your values more fully?
- Who or what are you grateful for in supporting your growth?
- How will you celebrate your journey and continue to acknowledge your growth moving forward?

Remember, the journey of personal growth is ongoing. There is no final destination, no point at which we are 'finished' growing. But by pausing to celebrate our progress and express gratitude for our experiences, we nourish ourselves for the ongoing adventure of life.

May you continue to grow, learn, and evolve throughout your life. May you meet each new challenge and triumph with an open heart and a curious mind. And may you always remember to celebrate your journey, acknowledging the courage, resilience, and beauty of your ever-unfolding self.

With deep appreciation for your presence on this journey,
Afarin

Part Four
Navigating Life's Triangle – Integration –

Chapter 13

Weaving It All Together: Living a Life of Validation, Acceptance, and Intention

Dear courageous traveler,

As we near the end of our journey together, it's time to step back and see the tapestry we've been weaving. Throughout this book, we've explored three fundamental practices: validating our truth, accepting what is, and moving forward with intention. Each of these practices is powerful on its own, but when integrated, they create a robust framework for living a life of authenticity, resilience, and purpose.

Let's revisit each practice and consider how they interweave:

Validation: Honoring Our Truth

We began by learning to validate our experiences and emotions, to listen deeply to our inner world without judgment. This practice of validation creates a foundation of self-trust and self-awareness. It allows us to acknowledge our feelings and needs, even when they're uncomfortable or inconvenient.

Acceptance: Embracing Reality

Building on this foundation of self-awareness, we then explored the practice of acceptance. We learned that accepting reality as it is doesn't mean we like it or approve of it, but rather that we stop expending energy fighting against what cannot be changed in the moment. This acceptance frees up our energy and allows us to see our situation more clearly.

Intention: Moving Forward with Purpose
Finally, we delved into the practice of living with intention. We clarified our values, aligned our actions with our deepest truths, and learned to navigate obstacles with perseverance and flexibility. This intentional living gives direction and meaning to our journey.

The Dance of Integration

Now, imagine these three practices as three strands of a braid. They are distinct, yet interconnected, each supporting and enhancing the others:

- Validation allows us to accept our true feelings about a situation, which in turn enables us to act with greater clarity and intention.
- Acceptance creates space for us to validate our experiences without getting caught in cycles of resistance, which frees us to move forward purposefully.
- Intentional action, grounded in our values, often requires us to validate difficult emotions and accept challenging realities along the way.

This integration is not a linear process, but a dynamic dance. Sometimes we may need to step back into validation when we find ourselves resisting reality. Other times, we may need to lean into acceptance when our intentions meet obstacles. The key is to remain flexible, to listen deeply to ourselves and our circumstances, and to respond with wisdom and compassion.

Practical Integration

Here are some ways to practice this integration in daily life:

1. **Morning Check-In**: Start your day with a brief check-in. Validate how you're feeling, accept your current circumstances, and set an intention for the day aligned with your values.

2. **Mindful Pauses**: Throughout the day, take brief pauses to practice this trio. Validate any emotions arising, accept the present moment as it is, and realign with your intentions if needed.

3. **Evening Reflection**: End your day by reflecting on how you've practiced validation, acceptance, and intention. Celebrate your efforts and consider how you might deepen your practice tomorrow.

4. **Challenging Situation Protocol**: When facing a difficult situation, consciously move through each practice. Validate your feelings about it, accept the reality of what is, and then consider how to respond in alignment with your values.

5. **Journaling**: Use writing as a tool to integrate these practices. You might structure your entries around "What I'm feeling" (validation), "What is" (acceptance), and "What I choose" (intention).

Remember, integration is an ongoing process. There will be times when you feel all three practices flowing seamlessly, and other times when you struggle to embody even one. Be patient with yourself. Each moment is an opportunity to begin again, to reconnect with your inner truth, to accept life as it is, and to move forward with purpose.

As we prepare to close our exploration together, I invite you to reflect on how these practices have shown up in your life so far. How has validating your experiences shifted your relationship with yourself? In what ways has acceptance brought you peace? How has living with intention aligned you more closely with your values?

In our final chapter, we'll extend this integrated approach to the broader context of social justice, exploring how these practices can support us in navigating and addressing the complexities of systemic inequalities.

With deep appreciation for your journey,
Afarin

Chapter 14

Navigating an Unfair World: Acceptance and Action
in the Face of Social Injustice

Dear compassionate seeker,

As we come to the final chapter of our journey, we turn our attention to a reality that often challenges our capacity for acceptance and tests our commitment to intentional living: the profound unfairness and injustice that exists in our world.

From the accident of our birth location to the long-standing systems of oppression that shape our societies, we are confronted daily with realities that can leave us feeling helpless, angry, or despairing. How do we reconcile our personal growth journey with the stark inequalities and injustices around us? How can we practice acceptance without falling into complacency, and take action without burning out?

Let's explore how the integrated practice of validation, acceptance, and intention can guide us in navigating these complex waters.

Validating Our Response to Injustice

The first step in addressing social injustice is to validate our emotional responses to it. It's natural and appropriate to feel anger, sadness, frustration, or despair when confronted with systemic oppression, environmental destruction, or gross inequalities. These emotions are not only valid but can serve as important catalysts for change.

Practice:

- Allow yourself to fully feel and acknowledge your emotions about social injustices.
- Share your feelings with trusted others, creating spaces for collective validation and support.
- Recognize that your emotional response is a reflection of your values and your connection to our shared humanity.

Accepting the Reality of Injustice

Acceptance in the face of social injustice doesn't mean approving of or resigning ourselves to these realities. Rather, it means acknowledging the truth of what is, right now, without getting lost in denial or wishful thinking. This clear-eyed acceptance is crucial for effective action.

We accept that:

- The world is fundamentally unfair in many ways.
- Change in complex systems is often slow and non-linear.
- We can't single-handedly solve all the world's problems.
- Our sphere of influence has limits, but it also has power.
    Practice:
- Cultivate awareness of global and local injustices without turning away.
- Practice self-compassion when feeling overwhelmed by the scale of world problems.

- Acknowledge the complexity of social issues, resisting the urge for oversimplified solutions.

Moving Forward with Intentional Action

Grounded in validation of our emotions and acceptance of reality, we can then move forward with intentional action. This action, rooted in our values and understanding of the situation, can take many forms:

1. **Education and Awareness**: Continuously learning about social issues and sharing knowledge with others.
2. **Personal Choices**: Aligning our daily decisions (consumption, interaction, etc.) with our values for social justice.
3. **Community Engagement**: Participating in local initiatives, mutual aid, or grassroots organizations.
4. **Advocacy and Activism**: Using our voice and resources to push for systemic changes.
5. **Professional Choices**: Bringing our values for social justice into our work and career decisions.
6. **Support and Allyship**: Standing with and amplifying the voices of marginalized communities.

Practice:
- Clarify your personal values regarding social justice.
- Identify areas where you have influence and can make a difference.
- Set realistic, sustainable goals for your engagement with social issues.
- Regularly reflect on and adjust your actions based on their impact and your capacity.

Balancing Acceptance and Action

The key to sustainable engagement with social justice is finding a balance between acceptance and action. We need acceptance to prevent burnout and to see clearly, but we need action to create change. This balance isn't static – it's a dynamic process of engagement, rest, reflection, and renewed commitment.

Remember:

- Change is possible, but it often happens slowly and incrementally.
- Every action, no matter how small, can contribute to a larger shift.
- Taking care of yourself is not selfish – it's necessary for sustained engagement.
- You're part of a larger movement; you don't have to do it all alone.

Embracing Complexity and Paradox

As we navigate social injustice, we often encounter paradoxes:

- We must accept the world as it is, yet work to change it.
- We need to acknowledge our privileges, yet not be paralyzed by guilt.
- We should be urgent about change, yet patient with the process.
- We must have hope for the future, while fully facing current realities.

Embracing these paradoxes – holding them with compassion and nuance – is part of the mature approach to social engagement.

A Personal Invitation

As we close this chapter and this book, I invite you to reflect on your place in the larger tapestry of human society. How can you honor your own journey of growth while also contributing to our collective flourishing? What unique gifts, perspectives, or resources can you bring to the work of creating a more just and equitable world?

Remember, you don't have to be perfect or have all the answers. What matters is your willingness to engage, to learn, to act with integrity, and to stay open-hearted in the face of both beauty and brokenness.

May you find the courage to face our world's injustices with clear eyes and an open heart. May you discover the unique role you can play in bending the arc of history towards justice. And may you always remember that your own healing and growth is intimately connected with the healing and growth of our entire human family.

With profound gratitude for your presence on this journey,

Afarin

Conclusion
Embracing the Fullness of Life

Dear friend,

As we come to the close of our journey together through these pages, I'm filled with a sense of gratitude and hope. Gratitude for the courage and openness you've brought to this exploration, and hope for the continued unfolding of your unique and beautiful path.

Throughout this book, we've explored the transformative practices of validation, acceptance, and purposeful action. We've delved into the power of embracing our imperfections, dancing with uncertainty, and persevering in the face of obstacles. We've discovered the importance of living our values, celebrating our progress, and cultivating gratitude along the way.

But perhaps the most important thread woven through all of these chapters is the invitation to embrace the fullness of life - with all its joys and sorrows, its triumphs and challenges, its moments of crystal clarity and periods of confusing ambiguity.

Life, in all its messy, beautiful complexity, is not a problem to be solved but a journey to be lived. It's my deepest hope that the ideas and practices we've explored together have equipped you with tools to navigate this journey with greater ease, authenticity, and joy.

As you move forward from here, remember:

- You are worthy of love and belonging, exactly as you are.
- Your feelings and experiences are valid, even when they're uncomfortable or inconvenient.
- You have the capacity to grow, learn, and evolve throughout your life.
- Your values can serve as a compass, guiding you towards a life of meaning and purpose.
- Challenges and setbacks are not failures, but opportunities for growth and learning.
- You are not alone - we are all connected in our shared humanity.
- Every small step towards living your truth matters and is worthy of celebration.

May you continue to grow in self-awareness and self-compassion. May you find the courage to live your values and share your unique gifts with the world. May you dance with uncertainty, embrace your imperfections, and celebrate your journey.

And always remember, you are enough. You matter. Your presence in this world makes a difference.

Thank you for sharing this journey with me. May your path forward be filled with growth, joy, and deep fulfillment.

With boundless faith in your unfolding,
Afarin

Appendix A
Additional Exercises and Practices

1. **Values Clarification Exercise**
   - List 50 things you love or enjoy
   - Identify themes among these items
   - Translate themes into core values
2. **Mindfulness Body Scan**
   - A guided 15-minute practice for body awareness and relaxation
3. **Self-Compassion Letter**
   - Write a letter to yourself from the perspective of a loving, compassionate friend
4. **Gratitude Scavenger Hunt**
   - List of items to find/photograph that you're grateful for in your daily life
5. **Values-Based Decision Making Framework**
   - A step-by-step guide for making decisions aligned with your values

Appendix B
Recommended Resources

Books:
1. "Self-Compassion" by Kristin Neff
2. "Daring Greatly" by Brené Brown
3. "Man's Search for Meaning" by Viktor Frankl
4. "Mindset" by Carol Dweck
5. "The Gifts of Imperfection" by Brené Brown
6. "Privilege, power, and difference" by Allen Johnson

Websites:
1. Greater Good Science Center (greatergood.berkeley.edu)
2. Mindful.org

Apps:
1. Headspace (for meditation)
2. Jour (for journaling)
3. Calm (for sleep and relaxation)

Appendix C
Workbook Section

Chapter 1: Validating Our Experiences
Reflection Questions:

    1.   When was the last time you felt truly heard and understood by someone? How did it make you feel?

    2.   In what situations do you find it most challenging to validate your own experiences?

    3.   How might your life be different if you consistently validated your own feelings and experiences?

Journaling Prompts:

    1.   Write about a time when you dismissed your own feelings. How would you respond differently now, using self-validation?

    2.   Describe a recent emotional experience in detail, without judgment. What were you feeling, and why might those feelings make sense given the situation?

Practice Exercise:

    1.   Self-Validation Mirror Exercise: Stand in front of a mirror. Speak aloud about a recent challenging experience. As you describe your feelings, practice validating them out loud. For example, "It's understandable that I felt anxious in that situation. My feelings make sense."

Chapter 2: Accepting What Is Mindfulness Exercise:

1. RAIN Practice (Recognize, Allow, Investigate, Nurture): Choose a current difficulty in your life. Practice the RAIN steps with it, especially focusing on the "Allow" step to cultivate acceptance.

Scenario for Practicing Acceptance:

1. Imagine you're stuck in heavy traffic and running late for an important meeting. Write out how you might practice acceptance in this situation, rather than resistance.

Self-Reflection Worksheet:

1. List three situations in your life that you're currently resisting. For each one, write:

   o What am I resisting?

   o What would acceptance look like in this situation?

   o What might I gain by practicing acceptance here?

Chapter 3: Moving Forward with Intention

Values Clarification Worksheet:

1. List 10 peak experiences in your life. What values were you expressing or fulfilling in those moments?

2. Imagine you're at your 80th birthday party. What would you want people to say about how you lived your life? What values do these aspirations reflect?

Goal-Setting Template:

1. Choose one of your top values. Set a SMART goal (Specific, Measurable, Achievable, Relevant, Time-bound) that would help you live this value more fully in the next month.

Action Plan Development Guide:

1. For the goal you set above, break it down into weekly actionable steps.

2. Identify potential obstacles to achieving this goal and brainstorm strategies to overcome them.

3. List three people or resources that could support you in achieving this goal.

Reflective Questions:

1. How aligned do you feel your current life is with your core values? Where do you see the biggest gaps?

2. What's one small change you could make this week to live more in line with your values?

3. How might your life look different in a year if you consistently made choices based on your values?

References

Brown, B. (2012). Daring greatly: How the courage to be vulnerable transforms the way we live, love, parent, and lead. Gotham Books.

Brown, B. (2010). The gifts of imperfection: Let go of who you think you're supposed to be and embrace who you are. Hazelden Publishing.

Dweck, C. S. (2006). Mindset: The new psychology of success. Random House.

Frankl, V. E. (1959). Man's search for meaning. Beacon Press.

Johnson, A. G. (2006). *Privilege, power, and difference* (2nd ed.). McGraw-Hill.

Neff, K. (2011). Self-compassion: The proven power of being kind to yourself. William Morrow.

Tao Te Ching. (n.d.). [Ancient Chinese text attributed to Laozi].

Greater Good Science Center. (n.d.). https://greatergood.berkeley.edu/

Headspace. (n.d.). [Mobile application software]. https://www.headspace.com/

Tippett, K. (Host). (n.d.). On Being [Audio podcast]. https://onbeing.org/series/podcast/

About the Author

Afarin Rajaei, Ph.D., LMFT, is a medical, marriage, and family therapist, educator, and researcher with a rich blend of Eastern and Western perspectives on mental health and personal growth. Born and raised in Iran, Dr. Rajaei moved to the United States in her early twenties, where she earned a Ph.D. in Medical Family Therapy. She maintains a private online practice, teaches at a university, and contributes valuable insights to the field through her research on culture, family dynamics, and well-being. She is the author of "Match Me If You Can!," an educational game for relationships. Dr. Rajaei's work is driven by her belief in the resilience of human beings and the transformative power of self-compassion, mindfulness, and purposeful living. Her unique approach combines evidence-based psychological principles and systemic-holistic perspective with deep empathy and cultural insight, offering readers a path to more authentic and fulfilling lives.

Printed in the USA
CPSIA information can be obtained
at www.ICGtesting.com
LVHW091542221024
794497LV00002B/345